How To Line Up Your Fourth Putt

by Bobby Rusher

D0880055

𝓜 Meadowbrook Press

Distributed by Simon & Schuster
New York

Library of Congress Cataloging-in-Publication Data

Rusher, Bobby.
      How to line up your fourth putt / by Bobby Rusher.
      p. cm.
      ISBN # 0-88166-284-4 (Meadowbrook)
      ISBN # 0-671-52126-8 (S&S)
      1. Golf—Humor. I. Title.
    GV967.R87 1997
    796.352'02'07—dc21

                                                                97-5059
                                                                CIP

Editorial Coordinator: Liya Lev Oertel
Copyeditor: Kevin Frazzini
Production Manager: Joe Gagne
Production Assistant: Danielle White
Text Design: Amy Unger
Cover Art: Jeff Cornell
Illustrations: Cindy Davis

Published by Meadowbrook Press, 5451 Smetana Drive, Minnetonka, MN 55343

BOOK TRADE DISTRIBUTION by Simon & Schuster, a division of Simon and Schuster, Inc., 1230 Avenue of the Americas, New York, NY 10020

00 99 98 97   10 9 8 7 6 5 4 3 2 1

Printed in the United States of America

DEDICATION

This book was written for golfers who appreciate the simple pleasures of strange trajectories and the mysterious bounce, and who can laugh at deep divots and the big banana.

This book is dedicated to Andrew and Amy, who, someday, will learn to like this silly game.

TABLE OF CONTENTS

TABLE OF CONTENTS

TABLE OF CONTENTS

TABLE OF CONTENTS

TABLE OF CONTENTS

On Announcing Your Handicap

As we all know, the handicap system allows the highly handicapped golfer to enjoy a round with Greg Norman. Right, Greg?

It is of paramount importance, therefore, to know how to handle yourself when queried about your "handicaps." You must know how to mislead your opponent without feeling guilty because you lied.

When someone asks, "Well, what's your handicap?" you can say a number of things:

1. You can tell the truth and say, " I'm a thirty-six," and then proceed as usual to ruin what would otherwise have been a pleasant afternoon.

2. You can *subtract* thirty strokes from your actual handicap and announce you are a "six," but this is

not a money-making proposition, which is the whole point, right? Also, if you say you're a "six" and are therefore paired with a "twenty-four," your partner will put a nine-iron to your solar plexus by the third hole, because you are a *Complete Jerk*. (See Chapter 12.)

3. You can add thirty strokes to your handicap, thereby leading to the embarrassing prospect of having to grin and mumble, "I'm a sixty-six."

   You don't want to do this either, unless you are a *Complete Jerk*. (See Chapter 12.)

4. Your best response is to repeat the old joke: "I usually shoot in the eighties; but if it gets any colder than that, I don't play at all." You will anger a lot of serious golfers with this one, but, using techniques discussed later, you'll make money no matter what they think. Screw 'em.

P.S. Also never "plumb bob" your putts if you lie more than ten on the green. (You may well be a *Complete Jerk* already! See Chapter 12.)

Note: Under scenario 2 or 3, whatever happens, you just say, "I'm just no good at math," at the end of the round, and quickly buy a round of drinks for the entire membership.

How To Line Up Your Fourth Putt

OK. This method never fails. (Provided your third putt left you no more than six feet from the cup.)

1. Grab your putter.
2. Walk once slowly around the perimeter of the green mumbling the word "POO-POO-KAH-KAH" over and over, holding your club at arm's length in front of you. This is the beginning of the ceremony.
3. Stop and button your collar all the way to the neck.
4. Stand over the ball and look up at the sky. Raise your putter into the air with both hands and say, "This, by God, is it!"
5. Slowly look down at your ball. It will be about two feet from the hole!

6. Remember all the things you did wrong in life, keeping your chin on your chest.

7. Say "POO-POO-KAH-KAH" tightly one more time. Your ball will now be about one foot from the hole.

8. Step back, breathe deeply and drop to your knees, "reading" the green intensely. Quietly and gently say, "Aw, sheee . . . it."

9. Stand up! Throw your putter down and violently tear open the Velcro seal on your golf glove! Heave the glove into the nearest bunker. You will feel a serenity like none you've ever known.

10. Your ball will now be seven inches from the cup.

11. Now nestle that putter into your left hand, forming a "V" where your thumb and index finger collide. Imagine a long sharp stake running from the ball, through the clubhead, past the elbow, into the heart and, finally, piercing the brain. That's it! This is the real beginning of the stroke itself, when ball, club, hands, heart and brain are all connected by a long, sharp stake.

12. Cover your left hand by wrapping it with your right hand from the opposite side.

13. You should now be breathing heavily and whispering "POO-POO-KAH-KAH" softly but quickly. Your ball will be two inches from the cup.

14. Putt the damned thing in! If you miss, say "POO-POO-KAH-KAH" one more time.

CHAPTER 2

How To Hit A "Dunlop 2" From The Rough On Your Second Shot, When You Hit A "Titleist 1" From The Tee

To accomplish this without being penalized, you need Drop Pocket Golf Slacks. (See Chapter 10.) Basically, you feign an intense search for the lost Titleist, then drop the Dunlop silently using your new slacks. Simultaneously yell, "I found it!"

The key here is that you must be sure *nobody* knows what you actually hit from the tee. Be sure to tee your ball so that identifying marks, labels, numbers and logos are *all on the bottom of the ball.*

4

CHAPTER 3

When To Chip From The Tee

When? Well,

1. When you already lie six on that tee.
2. To demonstrate that your power and control are totally independent of the club you use.
3. To get back to the fairway (because to get to this tee, you sliced an approach to the third).
4. When you're playing with a *Complete Jerk*. (See Chapter 12.)

When Trajectory Is Important On Short Putts

Trajectory is important on short putts:

1. If you wish to enter the hole directly, without touching the rim of the cup at all, as in "slam dunk" or "swish" shots. (If you achieve this, please be sure to yell "SWISH" so your opponents know you meant it.) You may need to do this (to "slam dunk" a putt):

   a. When your opponent's ball is in front of yours.

   b. When funds have been escrowed against the possibility of your actually executing the shot.

   c. When you want to keep your balls absolutely clean.

2. If the putt is over ninety yards long.

3. When you attempt to throw the ball into the cup, to forestall otherwise suicidal or homicidal behavior, because you lie eight on a par-three green.

The Art Of Cleaning Your Balls When Your Opponent Is On The Tee

This is a great ploy, another certain money-maker. Feign innocence and apology, but clean your ball loudly whenever you need to screw up your opponent's drive. He'll be upset, but most players won't go so far as to say anything; and for those who do comment, you can resort to alternative techniques described in other chapters. By the time most players actually complain, they've already lost five strokes! They'll get over it.

CHAPTER 6

How To Avoid The Water When You Lie Eight In The Bunker

Pick up.

How To Get More Distance Off The Shank

This can be guaranteed by modifying your clubs the next time you have them re-gripped. Just ask your pro to attach two inches of grip material on the lowest part of the shaft, where shaft meets head, *where ball meets shank.* The hard rubber will double your normal shank yardage, known as "shankage."

CHAPTER 8

How To Achieve The Flawless Swing Without Injuring Yourself Or Loved Ones

This requires simple movements, the main goal of which is to avoid hurting your left leg, or damaging your partner's forehead. The flawless swing is easy:

Make sure on the backswing that your armswing stretches the left half of your body around your right leg, which should be completely stationary at all times. If you're left-handed, ensure that your rightswing pulls your backswing to the other side of your body, shifting one-third of your weight through the entire swing, until the end.

Otherwise, you'll miss the ball . . . or hurt somebody.

CHAPTER 9

How To Use Your Shadow To Maximize Earnings

Shadow play is very, very effective on the greens, especially early in the morning or late in the afternoon when long shadows allow you to interfere with your opponent's putting while still standing yards away, pretending to be polite. Only slight movement at the proper moment can turn a birdie three into a bogey five. This technique was used to great advantage twice in the first round of the seventh Bogey Four Open. Those who were there still talk about it. Especially George.

(A) * HIDDEN IN GLOVE IS TINY REMOTE CONTROL DEVICE EMITTING FREQUENCY WHICH ACTIVATES LEVER

* CAUTION! WHEN WEARING THIS FOXKELS® GARMENT IS ON, ALL MICROWAVE APPLIANCES.

(B) LEVER RELEASES BALL ONE-AT-A-TIME HIDED BY GRAVITY, BALL DROPS TO GROUND

(C) BALL ROLLS TO POSITION

Where To Buy Golf Pants With "Drop Pockets"

Most people know about special shoes and gloves in the game, but do not normally become aware of the existence (and great utility) of other clothing until quite late in their careers.

My buddy Ernie was playing in '83 with a thirty-six handicap and was considered a valuable asset by his Partner. Partner was a good golfer, a serious golfer (a pain in the ass).

One day on the second hole, Ernie delivered a blow which sent his tee shot screeching low into the woods, far left, about 120 yards out. Partner screamed that they *had* to find that ball because Ernie got two strokes on the hole, etc.

The foursome looked in vain, but Partner stayed behind to continue the search. When Ernie was about fifty yards away, Partner yelled that he had found the ball! Ernie couldn't believe it; but when he returned to the area, the ball was there, brilliant in the sun, softly sitting atop a small mound of grass, in the middle of a dirt road. A clear shot to the green. Partner was truly pleased and grinned widely. Ernie whispered that he had hit a Titleist and that this was a Dunlop. Partner said, "Shut up and swing." So he did. Four net two. Great game, golf.

Partner later divulged the address of a store in Miami where Drop Pocket Golf Slacks are available.*

* Send your pants and $100 to the author if you can't find a pair. Your slacks will be returned with pockets "dropped" and ready for score-lowering wear.

CHAPTER 11

How To Score Well At Night

Nighttime golf is becoming very popular at certain clubs in New Jersey. Cooler, less crowded, and only slightly more dangerous for most players, successful play in the dark requires observance of just a few key rules:

1. You must wear your Drop Pocket Golf Slacks (see Chapter 10) because they are most helpful at night (for obvious reasons).

2. Bring a kazoo, whistle, or other noisemaker to help identify your position to other players.

3. *Never* let anyone play through.

4. Concentrate on "feel."

5. "Hear" the ball into the cup.

CHAPTER 12

Proper Etiquette When You're Playing With A Complete Jerk

Certain golfers have the revolting habit of continually explaining the rules of the game and the proper etiquette for each and every situation, and of reviewing your swing for you after every stroke. These people average 103. When dealing with this kind of player, do this: Deliver a nine-iron to the solar plexus, on about the third fairway. This is an extremely effective way to communicate your feelings concerning his advice, and will preclude further critical or instructional comment.

Crying And How To Handle It

It is hard to maintain the proper attitude in the game of golf, to have a sense of humor. It is easy, once you are "hooked," to believe that you are better than you are, that the shanked four-iron was an aberration. Getting mad, while ugly and unpleasant for your partner, is easy to understand. Indeed, crying is perfectly reasonable.

But it doesn't help your game. Peter, a great athlete and a rational man, put this all in perspective. His friend Jeffrey was convinced that he was finally "getting" this game, so when, in the eighth Bogey Four Open, Jeff sliced a drive into the water on the second hole, he was indignant, visibly agitated, and extremely unfriendly. He was crying.

As they left the tee, Peter walked with Jeffrey and asked him if he considered himself a good golfer. Jeffrey stammered, "Naw, not really, well, of course not," and Peter simply asked: "Then what are you so pissed off about?"

The Best Time To Tell Jokes

Joke-telling on the golf course is usually okay at the tee, while waiting for the foursome ahead of you, or while walking toward your ball. To make money, though, you must beak this general rule and tell jokes while your opponent attempts to extract himself from a hazard, or just after he has entered the hazard.

It is also important to laugh at your *own* jokes, especially when telling them to upset your opponent. A great laugher is the one about the flamenco dancer and the rooster. Excellent golf story.

CHAPTER 15

How To Rationalize A Seven-Hour Round

I played with my boss once. He was patient and kind, even though the round took six hours. At the bar, he explained that the next time I suggest a game of golf to anyone I should say, "Would you like to play golf for about four hours?" instead of, "Let's play a round."

The way to rationalize long rounds like this, or golf in general, is always to be in a position to say it was "business." This works extremely well with wives, and other superiors. (See Chapters 19 and 37.)

CHAPTER 16

What To Do When You've Parred The Course By The Eleventh Hole

It's best never to realize that it's possible to "reach par" after eleven holes. Many say that the only thing they regret about taking up the game so late in life is that they will never par a golf course. But it's merely a question of *when* you achieve par on a given course.

If you've parred by the eleventh, it's best to adopt an attitude of serenity, to enjoy the physical beauty around you, and to focus on the peaceful tranquility of golf. (Read Chapters 13, 18, and 36 for further insights.) Then break the club across your knee.

How To Find A Ball That Everyone Else Saw Go Into The Water

This is a tough one. Just deny it and use Drop Pockets to find your ball in the middle of the fairway.
(See Chapter 10 again.)

When To Blame The Caddie

Caddies can be blamed for almost everything.

For example:

1. The ball is lost because the caddie didn't watch it.

2. You shanked your three-iron because the caddie moved.

3. You overshot the green because the caddie chose the wrong club.

4. You missed the putt because the caddie read the green incorrectly.

5. You quit the game because your caddie suggested it.

CHAPTER 19

Why Your Wife No Longer Cares That You Birdied The Fourth (or . . . "frankly, sweetie, I don't give a damn")

The degree of indifference to success on the golf course varies widely from spouse to spouse, but basically she no longer cares because:

1. She's tired of hearing about it.

2. She knows you're lying anyway.

3. You play golf and ignore your primary responsibilities.

4. You've become a complete and utter fool.

5. She birdied it last week three times.

So, if you birdie the fourth, don't mention it.

How To Drive A Golf Cart When You're Two Down And Three To Go

In this situation, it is important to be the driver. That is, it has to be you behind the wheel, not your partner or opponent. You must therefore get to the cart *first* after you've made your fourth putt. If necessary, you must run, even though it is embarrassing, to beat the competition to the cart.

Having achieved this, the following is suggested:

1. *Crash* into the other carts. Always say, "God, I'm sorry, George. The pedal stuck."

2. *Back* into an opponent's cart. This usually will shake the bags loose as well, so you can unnerve

an entire foursome this way.

3. *Turn* the key to "reverse" position—the buzzing noise is great—just before an opponent's putt or drive.

You will think of many more maneuvers, like spin-outs, roll-outs, two-wheelers, glide stops, etc.

How To Let A Foursome Play Through Your Twosome Without Getting Embarrassed

This is not possible. If you have to do this, don't play for two weeks. Then give up the game entirely. In shame.

The "Double-Hit" And When To Use It

Also known as the "Tee See Chin" maneuver, the double-hit can be a real aid in those situations when your first contact with the ball is poor. The double-hit is very difficult off the drive, but can be easily accomplished with the wedge. The key is to make the secondary contact with the ball as soon as possible after you've realized how badly you've hit the ball in the first place. Otherwise your opponents will notice the maneuver and try to add strokes to your score, which is totally antithetical to the primary intent of the double-hit, which is to *lower* your score.

Be deft, and quick.

CHAPTER 23

How To Duck Hook From The Bunker And Still Get Home In Ten

You can do this, really. It just takes proper attitude. Your mom tried to give you proper golf attitude, even though neither you nor she realized it, when she used to say: "Brush your teeth" and "clean your room." If you had done these things in the first place, you probably wouldn't lie eight in the bunker.

So ask your mother.

The Insignificance Of Proper Grip

There are many, many people who buy the "latest" woods, experimental irons, new-tech shoes, alloy equipment, and hydraulic lift bags at least once each season. They get their clubs re-gripped, cleaned, balanced, weighted, shortened, lengthened, beveled, polished, shined, and monogrammed. They take lessons, do sit-ups, buy full-length mirrors, read books on technique, watch videos, listen to cassettes in their sleep—all to acquire subliminal understanding of the perfect stroke. They take golf vacations and change their diets. They consult stress-management experts, do yoga, run twenty miles a week, squeeze spring-loaded grips, and walk all the time aerobically.

Their pro told them what the *proper grip* was and how important this was, along, of course, with how to maintain a *constant swing plane.*

But you *know* it's a hoax. At your level, pal, just practice as much as you can. Forget the grip. If you don't have it, face it: You're a terminal ninety and you'll *never* par a course, okay?

CHAPTER 25

Why You Should Always Leave The Course After Four Hours No Matter What Hole You're On

Why prolong the agony? Leave, go home, chop wood, drink beer. Don't stay on the course. Doing so is bad, very bad, changes your relationship with your friends and colleagues, and causes minor memory loss. So just quietly stroll away, no matter what hole you're on, after four hours, max! You'll be glad you did it.

How To Enjoy Your Partner's 129

This is one of the most difficult tasks in golf. First of all, if your partner is on his or her way to a 129, chances are that this poor soul is literally sick with embarrassment already, especially in view of the fact that everyone else in the foursome has probably ignored him completely for at least four holes. This person may even be crying, in which case, give him a copy of this book and point him to Chapters 13 and 25. If things get real bad, direct him to Chapter 30 or employ techniques outlined in Chapter 39.

In any event, enjoying someone else's mortification is difficult, but the best medicine is laughter.

So, when he slices again on the tenth to penetrate the sixty-stroke barrier a bit early, just laugh—hysterically. Ask the rest of the foursome, "Did you boys see that? Unbelievable!" See what happens. Hopefully your partner hasn't read Chapter 12.

The Importance Of Hysterical Laughter After The Banana Slice

If the banana slice is your partner's, this response will lead to a renewed relationship, an affirmation, hopefully, of trust and affection. If not, this will add at least a stroke to your opponent's game.

If the banana is yours, this response will divert the attention of the foursome from the actual location of your ball to focus on how to make you stop laughing. You will thus be able to "find" your ball more easily, using Drop Pocket Golf Slacks technology. (See Chapter 10.)

If the banana slice is your opponent's, he will spend the next twenty minutes trying to decide what to do to you, dropping at least five strokes in the process.

If the banana has been produced by your spouse . . . do not, under any circumstances, laugh. In fact, remain totally silent until your spouse decides to speak to you. Otherwise, awesome consequences will ensue. Awesome.

How To Relax When You're Hitting "Five Off The Tee"

There's a guy named George. Now I *know* that George cannot possibly shoot under 100. Nevertheless, I saw George one day and he said, "Hey, Bobby, I shot an eighty-five yesterday." I said, "Sure, George." He said, "No, I mean it, I really was *on!*" So I said, "Then let's play tomorrow." George said, "Okay." You see, he had really convinced *himself* that he had shot an eighty-five, and, long-term, such self-delusion is unhealthy, since it leads to broken thumbs and bad debts.

George slashed his way to the seventeenth, by which time, according to my card, he had accumulated 101 strokes (counting things like lost balls, out-of-bounds, and other events yielding additional strokes). I asked George what he had going into the last two holes, since I was considering an additional bet, having recorded 104 attempts at the ball myself. Stepping up to the tee, and very relaxed, George said, "I have seventy-three so far." I said, "Sure, George."

The seventeenth, par three, 190 yards, is "all carry," which means: do not top it, or hit it short, because there's nothing but water between the tee and green. So George concentrated completely and hit a four-iron seventy-five yards, maximum elevation two feet, forty-five degrees (on average) off-line, slice acceleration five feet per millisecond, one bounce on the water, and quickly thereafter to the bottom of the lake, far right. My stroke counter said George lay two.

George approached his bag, undaunted, still professional, silently concentrating, obviously having realized he neglected to compensate for the wind. He solemnly withdrew his three-iron from the bag and gently dropped his cigar near the back of the tee, preparing gravely for the next blow. The ball jumped two feet forward; the tee went into the water; a pound of turf spun out left. I felt that George lay four.

George took a confident puff on his cigar, and very slowly pulled out his driver. The ball sailed almost straight up, but on line, and, miraculously, three minutes later, came to rest forty-five feet from the pin, off the green, in the short rough.

George continued, and flubbed a chip. He three-putted: I sincerely thought that added up to "nine."

I said, "George, what did you get?" George said, "A five." I said, "Sure, George."

The whole time, George was *totally* relaxed. So the thing to learn here is, to relax when you're hitting five off the tee, you must *ignore* your real score. Don't start counting strokes until you successfully leave the tee with a good, strong shot.

Good, basic, money-making golf.

The Myth Of Proper Timing

Actually this is no myth! Timing is everything, in every aspect of your life, forever. If you have it, you can hit sixteen in regulation early in your career. Also, you can get rich in real estate.

(See Chapters 3, 5, 14, 18, 24, 28, 36, and 39.)

Replacing The Divots Of Your Life

No one has ever played the game of life without extracting a divot or two from the innocent and unsuspecting earth. Sometimes it's hard to repair these clumps of failure, the loamy mounds of major misses, particularly when poor shot selection and incompetent execution are continual problems in life for most of us, every single day.

There is a solution, thanks be to the Lord. Forget the debt; refuse the abuse. Ignore the hazards and bunkers of your job and responsibilities. Don't worry about the "daily divots" of existence.

Instead, consolidate! Adopt a single focus: *PLAY GOLF* and concentrate all your energy on answering the one important question: how to get home in five!

How To Quietly Tear Open The Velcro Seal On Your Golf Glove

There's no quiet way to do this. But its value and effect far outweigh the obnoxious sound of its execution. The "Velcro rip" is the best technique yet devised for doing in the opposition.

"RRRIP"

The Importance Of Realizing That Most Golfers Are Bad Golfers

Ever play Pebble Beach? The first time you do, if it's early in your career as a high-handicap golfer, you will be intimidated. This is because you think you will embarrass yourself on one of the world's great golf courses. Because you haven't yet realized that most golfers are bad golfers.

The day I shot 141 at Pebble Beach, there was a mixed foursome in front of us and a foursome from Japan behind. The "Happy Couples" took six hours to get around; and the "Kioto Fore" never had a chance to play through—they took *seven* hours. See? They were all bad golfers, just like us, just like 99 percent of the people at Pebble Beach that day, like most people who play the game. Thank God.

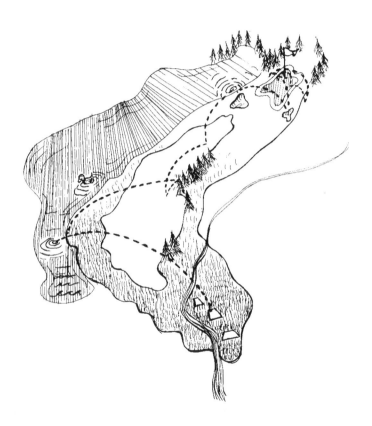

How To Walk A 6,500-Yard Course In Less Than 12,500 Yards

Play St. Andrews in Scotland—God's own natural golf course—Mecca. You will be thrilled to play where Henry VIII used to chip and putt.

One great caddie there is eighty-six years old. His name is Billy. I shot an eleven on the first hole and was obviously concerned, but Billy told me about Mr. Jeepers. Mr. Jeepers played the previous day and shot a forty-one on the first hole; and it got worse. At round's end, Jeepers asked Billy how caddies were paid at St. Andrews. Billy replied that he was paid by the round, but that he wished he were paid by the "yardage." Mr. Jeepers asked why this was, and Billy said: "Because, laddie, today I've been on every goddamn square yard of this course!"

So if you're going to walk 12,500 yards, ask for Billy. He'll ease your pain with comforting stories. He'll charge you by the yard, but if you use techniques set out here and in the Final Chapter, you'll win the Nassau no matter how far you walk.

CHAPTER 34

God And The Meaning Of The Double Bogey

Simple: The Double Bogey is a test of faith, developed by the Almighty as an efficient way to separate scratch believers from faithless hackers. If you can withstand a life of Double Bogeys, a special seat awaits you in the Golf Cart of Heaven. If you can come to understand the deeper meaning of the Double Bogey, you will reap great rewards. You will play the Final Nine with a smile on your face, knowing that a "Wider World of Sports" shall witness your penultimate putt—and shall forgive the Divots of Your Life!

Amen.

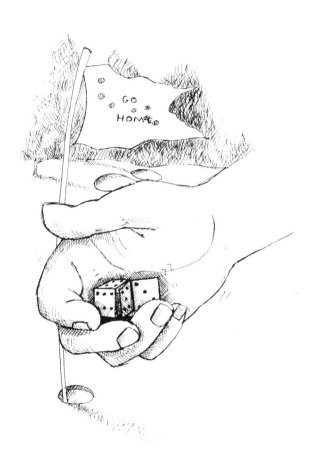

CHAPTER 35

When To Play Dice Instead Of Golf

When your handicap goes up two months in a row.

Profanity: How To Use It To Maximize Earnings On The Golf Course

Profanity is a natural inclination on the golf course, but its use must be goal-oriented. It is best to yell "Shit" or its equivalent not *after* you have swung your club, the most natural thing, but just *before* your opponent swings his. About 3 to 5 times a round. This is usually good for at least seven strokes.

CHAPTER 37

How Never To Pay For Another Golf Ball Again And Still Average 111

You never pay for golf balls, no matter how you play, if you are the chief financial officer of a large, publicly traded company. In this role, you play golf only "on business," and balls, dozens—with various logos—are handed to you before each round to induce you to buy goods and services from the generous giver.

So, try and become a CFO.

How To Feel Good About Yourself When Your Longest Lifetime Drive Was 117

How could anyone feel good under such circumstances? If you can't do better than 117, you are in the wrong sport.

Take up piano.

When To Suggest Swing Corrections To Your Opponent

The timing of Swing Correction Suggestions is obvious: whenever you're down by less than the number of holes left to play.

Why You Should Instruct Your Caddy To *Listen* For The Ball Off The Tee

If your handicap is great (i.e. greater than fifteen), which means your game is *not* great, remind your caddy that he won't find your tee shot by watching it. He must locate it instead by listening for it. For it is not possible to see the ball on its first acute, smokeless burst into the atmosphere, because your ball *never* begins its journey in the direction, nor at the angle or speed you intended. NEVER.

So instruct your caddy to listen: for the thud into the hillock twenty yards out, for the crack into the tree ninety yards out, for the plunk into the water 115 yards out, for the yelp of the dog 121 yards out, for the screech of automobile tires 130 yards out, for the scream of the woman on the adjoining tee ten yards back.

CHAPTER 41

What To Do When The Divot Weighs One And A Half Pounds, Has Traveled Twenty-Five Yards, And Your Ball Has Not Moved

Send the divot to the National Institute for the Study of Unnatural Phenomena, donate the ball to your caddy, throw your clubs (bag and all) into the nearest water hazard, remove your glove, bury it in the nearest bunker, throw your shoes gently into the deep rough . . . then slowly, silently, leave the course forever.

FOR CADDY

How To Choose A Caddy

This decision can be *very* important. Here's how to interview a prospective caddy:

You Whisper	He Replies
"I only have one ball in my bag today."	"I understand completely, sir. I have some extra balls in my pants."
"Are you wearing Drop Pocket Golf Pants?"	"Yes, sir."
"Buy 'em in Miami?"	"Yes, sir."
"Can you see well over long distances?"	"I have always found the ball hit by the person whose bag is across my shoulder, sir."

You Whisper

"Do you know that it is possible to have a good lie, even when you're in the woods?"

"How much is six plus seven plus five?

"Do you have change for a $50 bill?"

"Will you caddy for me today?"

He Replies

"I certainly do, sir. I find it happens often."

"Twelve, sir."

"I don't, sir. But I appreciate your predicament."

"Of course, sir."

See?

The Dot System Of Scoring

The Dot System of measuring performance on the golf course is really a form of modified Stableford scoring. It is actually the only way match competition should be scored in tournaments involving players with handicaps of twenty-two or more.

Basically, the system properly rewards the "highly handicapped" player whenever he is able to do anything correctly on the golf course, which is rare. It minimizes psychological depression, since even a round of triple bogeys might yield a dot or two.

So again, this system, which applauds you if you can manage to do anything right, gives you a "dot" for certain events, as follows. (You know what a "dot" is: a tiny circular mark on the card, made by stubbing the pencil directly at the card, point first, with a sharp, downward, vertical motion. Like a sand shot. Understand?)

Unsuccessfully teeing the ball:	- 3 dots
Teeing the ball without it falling off the tee:	+ 11 dots
Hitting the ball on the first try:	+ 2 dots
Hitting the ball on the second try:	+ 5 dots
Wearing color-coordinated slacks and shirt:	+ 3 dots
Wearing plaid slacks:	- 8 dots
Wearing rubber golf shoes:	- 5 dots
Wearing a baggy Hawaiian shirt:	- 8 dots
Keeping your shirt tucked in:	+ 10 dots

Wearing Drop Pocket Golf Slacks:	+ 15 dots
Slicing into the water:	- 10 dots
Hitting straight into the water:	+ 6 dots
Hitting it straight:	+ 2 dots
Hitting the fairway in the air off the tee:	+ 7 dots
Staying in the fairway off the tee:	+ 1 dot
Choosing the right club:	+ 2 dots
Choosing the wrong club:	- 1 dot
Staying out of the bunkers on a given hole:	+ 3 dots
Getting out of the bunker in less than three strokes:	+ 6 dots
Par:	+ 8 dots (+ 6 dots if done "in regulation")
Birdie:	+ 10 dots
Eagle:	+ 11 dots

Sandy:	+ 12 dots
Wedgy:	+ 13 dots
One putt a green:	+ 7 dots
Chip in:	+ 13 dots
Sinking your fourth putt:	+ 25 dots
Green in regulation:	+ 6 dots
Bogey:	+ 4 dots
Double bogey:	+ 3 dots
Triple bogey:	+ 2 dots
Reaching the green on your second shot on a par three:	+ 7 dots
Picking up the wrong ball:	+ 4 dots if it's an opponent's ball; - 10 dots if it's your partner's

Hitting the wrong ball: + 6 dots, if you hit it well

Finding more balls than you lost: + 9 dots

So, let's say your first hole of the day is a par five, 510 yards. The following chart illustrates a possible Dot scoring result assuming a certain performance against an opponent, and simultaneously accumulates the actual number of strokes:

You	Opponent	You		Opponent	
		Dots Earned	Cum Strokes	Dots Earned	Cum Strokes
1. You're wearing Drop Pocket Golf Slacks.	He's wearing plaid slacks.	+15	0	-8	0
2. Your shirt is tucked in.	He's wearing a baggy Hawaiian shirt.	+10	0	-8	0
3. You're wearing brand new leather golf shoes.	He's wearing rubber golf shoes.	0	0	-5	0
4. You do the "Velcro rip."	His ball falls off during tee-up.	0	0	-3	0
5. You say, "Sorry."	He says, "No problem."	0	0	0	0
6. You clean your ball, loudly.	He slices his drive into the water.	0	0	-10	2
7. You successfully tee up.	He is not smiling.	+11	0	0	2

You	Opponent	You		Opponent	
		Dots Earned	Cum Strokes	Dots Earned	Cum Strokes
8. You miss your first attempt completely.	He is smiling.	0	1	0	2
9. You slice your second attempt onto the fairway, 117 yards out.	He smiles and says, "That'll work."	+13	3	0	2
10. You smile.	He hits his second attempt 220 yards, hits rough first, ends up in the fairway.	0	3	+1	3
11. You hook your fourth shot into the left rough.	He says, "You'll be all right."	0	4	0	3
12. You put your cart in reverse and the buzzer sounds.	He shanks a three-iron into a tree.	0	4	0	4

You	Opponent	You		Opponent	
		Dots Earned	Cum Strokes	Dots Earned	Cum Strokes
13. You say, "You've still got a line on it."	He intends to kill you.	0	4	0	4
14. You smile.	He hits a five-wood safely forward, straight.	0	4	+2	5
15. You hit a career three-iron to the green, straight, and lie three feet from the hole.	He is totally stunned.	+2	5	0	5
16. You say, "I've never done that before!"	He says, "Bullshit!"	0	5	0	5
17. You are laughing hysterically.	He has just banana-sliced into the trap.	0	5	0	6
18. You say, "Sorry."	He just looks at you.	0	5	0	6

You	Opponent	You		Opponent	
		Dots Earned	Cum Strokes	Dots Earned	Cum Strokes
19. You mark your ball.	He just looks at you.	0	5	0	6
20. You say "Hello" loudly to a friend in a passing foursome.	He flubs his trap shot and throws his wedge at you.	0	5	0	7
21. You say, "Hey, it's only a game for Christsake!"	He just looks at you.	0	5	0	7
22. You smile.	He gets out of the trap to the green.	0	5	+6	8
23. You smile.	He putts two.	0	5	0	10
24. You putt three times.	He says, "Tough green, eh?"	0	8	0	10

You	Opponent	You		Opponent	
		Dots Earned	Cum Strokes	Dots Earned	Cum Strokes
25. You *Line Up Your Fourth Putt,* and sink it.	He slowly grabs his wedge, like a baseball bat, and just looks at you, red with rage.	+25	9	0	10
26. You say, "I'm one up."	He throws his bag into the water, his shoes into the rough, his gloves into the bunker, and leaves the course forever.	0	9	0	10
Totals		**+76**	**9**	**-25**	**10**

Golf: It's Just a Game!

Selected by Bruce Lansky

Bruce Lansky has hit a hole-in-one with this collection of clever golf quotes from such devotees of the game as Lee Trevino, Gerald Ford, Bob Hope, and many, many more. Illustrated with some of the funniest cartoons ever to appear in *Golf Digest* and *Playboy*.

Order Form

Qty.	Title	Author	Order #	Unit Cost (U.S. $)	Total
	Age Happens	Lansky, B.	4025	$7.00	
	Are You Over the Hill?	Dodds, B.	4265	$7.00	
	Best Party Book	Warner, P.	6089	$8.00	
	Dads Say the Dumbest Things!	Lansky/Jones	4220	$6.00	
	Familiarity Breeds Children	Lansky, B.	4015	$7.00	
	For Better And For Worse	Lansky, B.	4000	$7.00	
	How to Line Up Your Fourth Putt	Rusher, B.	4075	$7.00	
	Golf: It's Just a Game!	Lansky, B.	4035	$7.00	
	How to Survive Your 40th Birthday	Dodds, B.	4260	$6.00	
	Joy of Friendship	Scotellaro, R.	3506	$7.00	
	Joy of Grandparenting	Sherins/Holleman	3502	$7.00	
	Joy of Marriage	Dodds, M. & B.	3504	$7.00	
	Joy of Parenthood	Blaustone, J.	3500	$7.00	
	Lovesick	Lansky, B.	4045	$7.00	
	Moms Say the Funniest Things!	Lansky, B.	4280	$6.00	
	Over-the-Hill Party Game Book	Cooke, C.	6062	$3.95	
				Subtotal	
				Shipping and Handling (see below)	
				MN residents add 6.5% sales tax	
				Total	

YES! Please send me the books indicated above. Add $2.00 shipping and handling for the first book and 50¢ for each additional book. Add $2.50 to total for books shipped to Canada. Overseas postage will be billed. Allow up to four weeks for delivery. Send check or money order payable to Meadowbrook Press. No cash or COD's, please. Prices subject to change without notice. **Quantity discounts available upon request.**
Send book(s) to:

Name _____ Address _____

City _____ State ___ Zip _____ Telephone (_____) _____

P.O. number (if necessary) _____ Payment via: ❏ Check or money order payable to Meadowbrook Press

Amount enclosed $ _____ ❏ Visa ❏ MasterCard (for orders over $10.00 only)

Account # _____ Signature _____ Exp. Date _____

A *FREE* Meadowbrook Press catalog is available upon request.

Mail to: Meadowbrook Press
5451 Smetana Drive, Minnetonka, MN 55343

Phone (612) 930-1100   Toll-Free 1-800-338-2232   Fax (612) 930-1940